REAL WORLD ECONOMICS™

How the World Bank

and the International Monetary Fund

Work

Barbara Gottfried Hollander

ROSEN
PUBLISHING®
New York

Published in 2013 by The Rosen Publishing Group, Inc.
29 East 21st Street, New York, NY 10010

Library of Congress Cataloging-in-Publication Data

Hollander, Barbara, 1970–
How the World Bank and the International Monetary Fund work/
Barbara Gottfried Hollander.—1st ed.
    p. cm.—(Real world economics)
Includes bibliographical references and index.
ISBN 978-1-4488-6787-5 (library binding)
1. World Bank—Juvenile literature. 2. International Monetary Fund—
Juvenile literature. 3. Development banks—Juvenile literature. I. Title.
HG3881.5.W57H65 2013
332.1'52—dc23

                                                                    2011045466

Manufactured in the United States of America

CPSIA Compliance Information: Batch #S12YA: For further information, contact Rosen Publishing, New York, New York, at
1-800-237-9932.

Contents

INTRODUCTION

In the 1940s, many governments struggled to rebuild their countries following World War II and the economic depression of the 1930s. Nations were in debt and realized that working together in the global economy could help reduce further economic hardships. In 1944, forty-four governments met in Bretton Woods, New Hampshire, to create a plan for the world economy. Part of this plan was forming the World Bank and laying the groundwork for an organization called the International Monetary Fund (IMF).

This important conference was aimed at stabilizing the world economy. It envisioned the IMF as the organization mainly responsible for this task. At that time, the World Bank consisted of only the International Bank for Reconstruction and Development (IBRD). The IBRD's responsibilities included lending, encouraging investment, supporting trade, and working with other international lending agencies. The

The International Monetary Fund's headquarters includes two buildings. Visitors to the IMF must obtain a guest pass by presenting photo identification and undergoing security screening.

United States was instrumental in offering financial assistance and providing the framework for both the World Bank and the IMF.

Throughout the decades, the structures and responsibilities of these international organizations have evolved. The focus of the World Bank and the IMF has shifted from helping war-torn countries to promoting economic and social development in the world's poorest nations. In today's world, many people confront life-threatening illnesses, lack of food and water, and limited opportunities for medical treatment and education every day. People worldwide also suffer from natural disasters, wars, and economic crises. In the spirit of the new Millennium Development Goals of the United Nations, the World Bank and International Monetary Fund are here to help.

CHAPTER ONE
THE WORLD BANK AND THE INTERNATIONAL MONETARY FUND

B oth the World Bank and the International Monetary Fund are part of the United Nations. Founded after World War II, the United Nations made official goals that included encouraging world peace, facilitating cooperation between countries, and helping the world's poor. The World Bank and IMF were established to help achieve these goals.

WORKING FOR THE WORLD BANK AND THE IMF

The World Bank is headquartered in Washington, D.C., and consists of 187 member countries. It has more than ten thousand employees in one hundred offices throughout the world. These employees include economists, environmental scientists, engineers, and educators. Three thousand of the bank's employees work in developing countries.

According to the World Bank, developing countries have low-to-middle standards of living; a standard of living is the comfort level provided by the availability of the goods and services. For example, the United States has a high standard of living because most Americans have goods (like food) and services (like doctors' visits and haircuts) relatively easily available to them. There are five high-income countries that the World Bank also classifies as developing countries because of their economic structures. The bank reports that over 80 percent of the people in the world live in developing countries.

Like the World Bank, the International Monetary Fund was formed at a 1944 United Nations conference in Bretton Woods, New Hampshire. The fund is also headquartered in Washington, D.C., and has 187 countries as members. But the

The 1944 Bretton Woods Conference was officially known as the United Nations Monetary and Financial Conference.

IMF is smaller than the World Bank, with only about 2,500 employees representing 160 countries.

Most of the fund's employees work in Washington, D.C., although the IMF also has offices in Paris, France; Geneva, Switzerland; and New York. Unlike the World Bank, the fund's employees do not work in developing countries, and they are mostly experts in economics and finance.

Being on the Same Page

The World Bank and the International Monetary Fund meet regularly to create growing economies with rising standards of living. The Development Committee gives suggestions to both organizations on helping low-income countries. There are also yearly meetings with the IMF's board of governors and the World Bank, where countries have the opportunity to talk about important issues in the world economy and what they mean to them. These meetings also encourage the board of governors to formulate plans to address these issues.

For example, suppose that a country is in debt and its economy is not growing. There are many issues for this country that the board of governors needs to figure out, like how will the country repay its debt? How can a country promote economic growth? And how will this debt affect the standard of living? One country's economic problems can also cause many issues for other countries. For example, the U.S. recession that began in December 2007 caused millions of people around the world to lose their jobs, homes, and money. So when the board of governors makes decisions for one country, it affects other countries, too.

Running the Bank and the Fund

Both the World Bank and the International Monetary Fund have structures that help them achieve their goals. The World Bank has a president and a board of executive directors that carry out the jobs of the bank. Each country has a share, or part, in the World Bank. The five countries with the most shares are the United States, the United Kingdom (England, Northern Ireland, Scotland, and Wales), France, Germany, and Japan. These countries each choose one of the twenty-four executive directors, all of whom serve two-year terms. The other nineteen executive directors come from different countries.

The highest level of the IMF's structure is called the board of governors. The board has one main governor and then alternate governors from the member countries. The board of governors gives a lot of the IMF's decision-making powers to its executive board. The IMF also has two committees that play important roles in the organization. The International Monetary and Financial Committee (IMFC) examines issues in the world economy and how the IMF can help. The Development Committee gives advice to both the IMF and the World Bank about the progress in developing countries.

Parts of the World Bank

The World Bank has a more complex structure than the IMF. Today, the bank consists of two institutions: the International Bank for Reconstruction and Development (IBRD) and the International Development Association (IDA). Both the IBRD and the IDA work together toward inclusiveness and sustainable globalization. The IBRD focuses on lowering

Visitors to the World Bank learn about its history, mission, and development. These briefings meet on various Tuesdays and Thursdays throughout the year.

poverty in eighty-six middle-income countries. According to an Independent Evaluation Group (IEG) review, 40 percent of the world's poor live in middle-income countries, with almost half of the people living in China. The IBRD also focuses on helping creditworthy poorer countries (such as Pakistan).

The goal of the IDA is to reduce poverty in the poorest countries of the world, where most people have less than $1,000 to live on for a whole year. For example, in the African country of Liberia, per capita income is only $190. Can you imagine surviving on less than $200 for the whole year? You would not be able to afford a place to live and food. In fact, most doctors' visits cost more than that without insurance.

How the World Bank Groups Countries

The World Bank groups countries mostly according to a measurement called the gross national income per capita. Gross national income (GNI) includes the total value of final goods and services made in a country, like cars, computers, clothes, and haircuts. It also adds in the net income from assets abroad, such as the income earned by an American storeowner from her clothing shop in London. Finally, GNI subtracts indirect business taxes (or sales taxes).

To find gross national income per capita, economists divide a country's GNI by the number of people in the country. Then, the World Bank uses per capita income to classify the poverty level of a country's population.

While countries define their own "poverty lines" (being below a poverty line usually refers to not having enough income to afford basic needs, like food, housing, and clothing), the bank groups its member countries, along with other economies that have more than thirty thousand people, into four groups:

- The low-income countries have a GNI per capita of $1,005 or less. Many of these countries are found in Africa, including Ethiopia, Madagascar, and Zimbabwe. According to the World Bank, Africa had 839.6 million people (about 2.5 as many as the United States) with a per capita income of $1,127 in 2010.
- The lower middle-income countries have an income per capita between $1,006 and $3,975, and upper

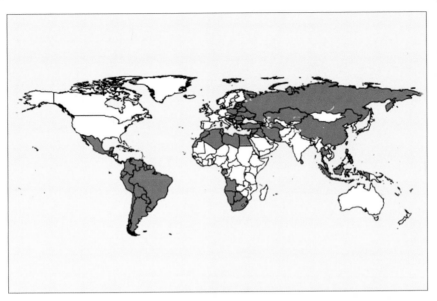

This World Bank map displays the middle-income countries (MICs) in red. These eighty-six countries are classified as MICs according to the bank's World Development Indicators.

middle-income countries range from $3,976 to $12,275. Also called developing economies, lower and middle-income countries include India, Egypt, Sudan, and Vietnam, as well as most countries in South America, like Brazil, Argentina, and Chile.

- High-income countries have a per capita income of at least $12,276. The United States, Japan, Israel, and many European countries (like the United Kingdom, Germany, Spain, and Italy) are high-income countries. In 2010, the United States had a GNI per capita of $47,140 and ranked eighteenth among high-income countries.

WORKING TOGETHER

Pascal Lamy is the fifth Director-General of the World Trade Organization. A native of France, Lamy was appointed in September 2005.

The World Bank is part of the World Bank Group. This group includes three other agencies: the International Finance Corporation, the Multilateral Investment Guarantee Agency, and the International Centre for Settlement of Investment Disputes. The goal of all of these organizations is to reduce poverty around the world. On July 1, 2007, Robert B. Zoellick began a five-year term as president of the World Bank. He is also the president of the World Bank Group.

Likewise, the International Monetary Fund works closely with other international organizations, such as the World Trade Organization (WTO). Both the IMF and the WTO strive to create a cooperative environment for countries to cooperate in the world economy. More economic interaction between countries can help reduce poverty and achieve higher standards of living.

CHAPTER TWO

JOBS OF THE IMF AND THE WORLD BANK

The original goals of the International Monetary Fund and the World Bank focused on the events that surrounded their creations in 1944, specifically not repeating the economic mistakes of the past and rebuilding war-torn countries after World War II. Later, the goals of these organizations evolved, as the needs of the world economy shifted.

COOPERATION, INTERNATIONAL TRADE, AND EXCHANGE RATES

At the 1944 United Nations Monetary and Financial Conference in Bretton Woods, 730 representatives from 44 countries decided the goals for a new organization called the International Monetary Fund. According to the Articles of Agreement, one goal of the IMF is to encourage international monetary cooperation. This means countries work together in matters that involve money. For example, the IMF's Development Committee arranges for countries to discuss economic issues and then offers its advice.

In 2010, Japan's gross domestic product was $730.1 billion. An estimated $4.31 trillion of total output were exports, such as Toyota cars sold to the United States.

Another original IMF goal is to encourage the growth of international trade. Trading between countries involves imports and exports. Imports are goods and services bought from other countries, like when Americans buy Japanese cars. Exports are goods and services sold to other countries, such as American companies selling computers to England. Exports add to a country's total production of goods and services. They also put more money into the economy, which helps a country's economy to grow.

Following the global recession of 2008–09, the World Bank Group (WBG) presented its first official trade strategy for 2011–2021. In its report, "Leveraging Trade for Development and Inclusive Trade," the WBG states, "No country in the last 50 years has sustained high levels of growth and significantly increased per capita income without greatly expanding trade." As part of its strategy, the World Bank Group focuses on four main areas. These areas include (1) encouraging trade competitiveness and export diversification (or making different goods and services for sale to foreign countries), (2) minimizing the effects of financial shocks, (3) lowering trade costs (like the costs of transportation) and improving trade logistics (like better border management), and (4) opening up more markets.

International transactions, like trading, involve different currencies (or money). When Americans buy toys, clothing, and furniture that are made in China, these transactions involve the U.S. dollar and the Chinese currency (called the yuan or renminbi). For international transactions to occur, businesses must have confidence that currencies are stable. They also need to know the exchange rate, or how much of one currency can be traded for another currency.

Stable exchange rates between different currencies encourage economic growth by increasing international transactions, such as trading goods and foreign investments.

Exchange rates can be fixed (remaining the same each day) or flexible (changing in response to the supply and demand for the currency). The IMF encourages countries to work together in the area of exchange rates—for example, keeping their currencies' values low to maintain favorable trade balances. The IMF discourages exchange rate moves like this because they give countries unfair trade advantages.

The IMF and the Bretton Woods System

When the IMF was first created, it maintained an exchange rate system known as the Bretton Woods system. This system linked the value of the U.S. dollar to the value of gold. American dollars could actually be traded for gold. The currencies of other countries were also linked to the U.S. dollar. But keeping a currency's value fixed is tricky because there are supply and demand forces that push the value of money to change constantly.

For example, when Canadians put their money into U.S. investments, their actions increase the demand for the American dollar. More demand for the dollar pushes the value of the American dollar to change. Under the Bretton Woods system, these pressures had to be balanced to hold the value of a currency steady. This was one of the IMF's jobs. It provided money for countries to borrow and use to counter these pressures.

Participating countries held some money with the IMF for this purpose. In 1971, the Bretton Woods system ended. The value of the U.S. dollar was no longer linked to gold or to the currencies of high-income countries. The IMF's job of maintaining this exchange rate system was gone.

IMF's Surveillance Tools

The International Monetary Fund uses three main tools to achieve its goals of monetary cooperation, financial stability, and sustained economic growth with poverty reduction. These tools include surveillance, financial assistance, and technical assistance. Member countries benefit from these tools, as they encourage their economies to grow and to avoid financial crises (like going bankrupt or being unable to pay the bills).

The IMF carries out surveillance on its member countries. This means that it examines the countries' economic and financial policies, like what the government spends money on and how much it spends. One condition of being an IMF member is allowing others (like the IMF and other countries) to know about these policies. The IMF conducts both bilateral and multilateral surveillances. Bilateral surveillance is where IMF employees meet with country leaders who affect the economy, such as business leaders, government officials, and representatives of workers (like unions). Then, the IMF gives advice on how to encourage economic growth and sustainable development.

Multilateral surveillance involves watching the activities and goals of a region, or group of countries. It also encourages monetary cooperation by helping organize regional conferences that promote economic growth and stability in a particular area. The IMF works with other organizations to monitor its countries. For example, the Financial Sector Assessment Program through the World Bank also looks at different parts of the economy and makes suggestions about how to help an economy avoid risks.

IMF's Financial Assistance

The International Monetary Fund provides financial assistance to countries with current or future balance of payments problems. Each country has a balance of payments, or record of international transactions. This record is kept over a certain period of time, like every year or every three months (quarterly). It includes the current account, capital account, and financial account. A balance of payments problem occurs when a country cannot find a way to pay expenses owed to other countries, while still keeping enough money in the bank (called reserves).

If a country has or might have a problem with its balance of payments, it can apply for a loan by submitting a "Letter of Intent" to the IMF's executive board. In this letter, a country usually commits to following future policies that will fix the balance of payments problems and allow the country to repay its loan. If the IMF agrees to provide a loan, money is given to the country in phases (over time), as the new policies are carried out.

The IMF gives loans to developing countries and to nations that have financial crises. The IMF also helps countries that are transitioning to market economies. In a market economy (like the United States), supply and demand for goods and services drive the economy. Some countries, like Russia, used to have planned economies, where the government made economic decisions (like the quantity and price of goods and services). As these countries become more market-oriented, the IMF helps out by providing loans.

The amount a country can borrow is often related to its quota. IMF countries have quotas that correspond to their

One of the functions of the IMF is to aid troubled economies. This woman walks through a near-empty grocery story in the now-defunct Soviet Union.

places in the world economy. These quotas make up most of the IMF's money. Some loans do not charge interest, while others have a cost of borrowing called the rate of charge. This interest rate is determined by the weekly interest rate of the Special

Drawing Rights (SDRs), a type of currency created by the IMF.

By lending money, the IMF can help its member countries address balance of payments problems and avoid or deal with financial crises. In return for these loans, the IMF requires countries to make policy changes that prevent future economic problems. These changes also allow countries to acquire the funds to repay their loans. The IMF has extended financial assistance to 80 percent of member countries at least one time.

IMF's Technical Assistance

When the IMF monitors a country's economy, it examines its fiscal, monetary, exchange rate, and financial policies. Fiscal policy refers to changes in government spending and taxes that are intended to affect a country's economic performance. For example, a government can spend more or less money. These spending changes affect how an economy grows and a country's debt. A country's central bank carries out monetary policy. This policy refers to changes in the growth of the money supply, which are meant to affect economic performance. By putting more or less money into the economy, a central bank can also affect the growth of a country.

257

14 10 1

BUYING RATES

SELLING RATE

		BUYING RATES	SELLING RATE
$		86.5000	86.800
€		7.19.800	72 180
£		136.000	138. 0
C.D$		85.0000	86.800
A.S$		84.6000	86.500
YEN		1.03600	1.2000

Currencies are bought and sold at currency exchange shops. Changes in a currency's rates can impact trade.

Exchange rate policy involves how a country manages the value of its currency compared to other currencies in the world. As mentioned, the value of a currency affects how countries interact with one another, especially in international trade. Finally, financial policy is about supervising and regulating a country's payment systems. Fiscal, monetary, exchange rate, and financial policies involve making decisions today that affect the economy in the future. Policy decisions are made based on what people expect to happen.

Balancing the effects of these policies is a challenging job. International organizations, like the IMF and the World Bank, suggest policies that help countries and regions achieve economic growth and poverty reduction, avoid economic troubles, and deal with financial crises. This help is called technical assistance. This assistance by the IMF also involves giving countries legal advice and aiding with the collection and organization of data, or statistics, like the gross national income per capita.

LENDING AND THE WORLD BANK

Originally, the World Bank provided loans to European countries that needed to rebuild after World War II. At that time, the World Bank was only the IBRD. Then, the World Bank grew to include the International Development Association (IDA) and became part of the World Bank Group. The World Bank Group is dedicated to reducing poverty around the world. So the World Bank shifted from mostly focusing on high-income countries in Europe to low- and middle-income countries in places like Africa, Asia, South America, Central America, and Europe.

The World Bank also offers two kinds of financial assistance: development policy funding and investment funding. Both types of funding aim to reduce poverty, support development, and encourage economic growth. Development policy funding (or adjustment loans) helps countries achieve policy goals. Investment funding is aimed at specific projects. For example, the World Bank provides money for education, health, and infrastructure (like roads). The IBRD provides loans, and the IDA gives credits (no-interest loans) and grants for investment funding. From 1990 to 2010, 75 to 80 percent of the World Bank's lending was investment funding.

Low-, middle-, and high-income countries can apply for financial assistance from the World Bank. The IDA provides grants and no-interest loans to low-income countries. In 2010, 40 percent of World Bank lending came from the IDA. Money borrowed from the IBRD must be repaid in fifteen to twenty years, with a three- to five-year grace period. Countries that do not repay these loans on time face suspension of new loans if thirty days late, and not receiving new loans if sixty days late. The IBRD receives most of its lending money by selling AAA-rated bonds to different countries. The IDA receives donations from forty countries every three years that it uses for grants and credits. In 2010, the IDA and the IBRD lent over $72 billion to developing countries.

Ten Great Questions
to Ask an Economist

1. Can I work for the World Bank or IMF?

2. How do I prepare for a job in the World Bank or IMF?

3. Can I make a donation to help the World Bank or IMF achieve its goals?

4. Does every country in the world belong to the World Bank and IMF?

5. How do the World Bank and IMF work together to reduce poverty?

6. Does every country that needs money receive a loan from these international organizations?

7. Do countries usually repay the loans that they receive from the IMF or World Bank?

8. Do high-income countries, like the United States, also receive aid from the World Bank or IMF?

9. How do these international organizations help a country's economy grow?

10. Can the IMF and World Bank prevent another global financial crisis?

CHAPTER THREE
AFFECTING NATIONAL ECONOMIES

The IMF and the World Bank perform vital roles in countries' economies. Their goals include encouraging balanced trade, exchange rate and financial stability, and monetary cooperation. By achieving these results, the international organizations help countries sustain economic growth, reach higher standards of living, and reduce poverty.

INTERNATIONAL TRADE AND MONETARY COOPERATION

Today, the IMF and the World Bank continue to encourage international trade. Trade is also an example of monetary cooperation because it involves countries working together to exchange goods and services for money. Increasing exports (or products sold to other countries) can help an economy grow because it puts more money into the economy. This can also raise a country's standard of living.

Suppose that an American shoe company sells its goods to Americans. The United States has a big market for shoes. Now,

In 2011, the most widely flown plane in the world was the Boeing Company's 737. This American company also makes the 787 Dreamliner, which is sold to customers such as Japan Airlines Corporation (JAL).

imagine that the American shoe company also sells to other countries (like Canada, Japan, and Germany). The shoe company has an even bigger market. By selling to more customers (at home and abroad), the shoe company earns even more revenue. It can also use its extra profits to make investments, like opening more factories and hiring more workers. This means that more people are joining the workforce, earning money, buying goods and services, and putting more money into the economy.

More money going into the economy is a sign of economic growth. When economists compare a country's output from consecutive time periods, they can tell if a country's economy is growing. A country's output is the total production of final goods and services (usually measured by the gross domestic product). A growing economy means that companies are selling more goods and services, earning more revenue, expanding their businesses, and hiring more workers. It also means more people are working and earning income that they can use to buy more goods and services. This results in an increased standard of living. So, a growing economy is good for consumers, producers, and the whole country.

The WBG report, "Leveraging Trade for Development and Inclusive Trade," noted, "More than 65 percent of Country Assistance Strategies include trade or trade-related activities." For example, trade in many African countries suffers from expensive transportation costs, border problems, and corruption. So, the World Bank provided $199 million for an East Africa Trade and Transport Facilitation Project. This project made it easier to transport goods between Kenya's port at Mombasa and countries inside Africa. According to the World Bank, trade at Mombasa grew almost 9 percent between 2006 and 2009. Uganda benefited a lot from this project, since 95 percent of its trade goes through Mombasa.

STABLE EXCHANGE RATES, FINANCIAL STABILITY, AND LENDING

The International Monetary Fund also encourages economic growth and higher standards of living by promoting both exchange rate and financial stability. Stable exchange rates and confidence in the currencies' values encourage countries to trade with each other. By monitoring and encouraging stable exchange rate systems, the IMF creates an environment that promotes trade and helps an economy grow.

Taking Apart the Balance of Payments

The balance of payments includes the current, capital, and financial accounts. The current account includes traded goods (like computers, clothes, and cars) and services (like tourism). This account also consists of money earned from foreign investments and the money earned while working in foreign countries (called workers' remittances). The capital account includes certain kinds of taxes, repayment of debt, and the cost of capital goods (or items used to make goods and services). The financial account includes money related to investments, gold reserves, and Special Drawing Rights (SDRs). The IMF issues Special Drawing Rights, which are international assets that can be used in the future. SDRs are like money in the bank that can be cashed in, when needed.

When the balance of payments is "in balance," the current account equals the capital account plus the financial account. Or, a country's credits (money received) equal its debits (money paid). But usually, this record of international transactions is not balanced. This means that a country can have a balance of payments deficit (money is owed to other countries) or a surplus (excess money is flowing in from other countries). A balance of payment deficit can indicate many problems within the economy, while a surplus can help an economy grow. In 2010, the United States had a balance of payments deficit. Countries with balance of payments surpluses included China, Japan, and Germany.

Suppose that a Chinese company exports clothes to America. These sales will result in more output (like gross domestic product, or GDP) for China and more money flowing into the Chinese economy. But what about America? What happens when Americans buy Chinese-made goods and money flows out of the American economy? In this case, some of the money flows back into the U.S. economy as investments. An investment is something that people put their money into because they hope to earn more money. Investments lay the foundation for future economic growth. When businesses invest in other countries, they are putting more money into other economies in hopes of receiving a return on their investment. In the case of the United States and China, China often buys U.S. government securities (like U.S. Treasury bonds) to help pay for America's debt.

Many physical investments are expensive, like building new factories. They require financing by credit, or borrowing money. Investors who lend this money must be confident that the investment will yield high returns (money earned from an investment). Investing in countries (like through government securities) requires confidence in a country's economic performance. By encouraging financial stability, the IMF helps countries create an environment of accessible credit and investments that form a basis for economic growth.

Unlike the IMF, which gives financial aid directly to countries, the World Bank also invests directly in projects intended to increase the standard of living, reduce poverty, and create sustainable development. These projects focus on areas such as the environment (like climate change and pollution management), human development (such as child health, HIV/AIDS, malaria, education, and nutrition), rural development (like the

Chinese companies manufacture many labor-intensive goods, such as textiles. These goods are exported to countries like the United States.

Global Food Crises), urban development, infrastructure, and social development.

For example, one project in the 1990s was to improve education in the African country of Ghana. A $50 million credit for Ghana's Basic Education Sector Improvement Project was intended to reduce poverty by allowing more people to obtain the skills needed for work. Although there were challenges, results

Anti-Corruption Measures and the World Bank

According to the World Bank Web site, "the Bank has identified corruption as among the greatest obstacles to economic and social development." Corruption, or dishonest behavior by people in control, tends to involve people working in the government and private businesses. Countries have formulated over six hundred programs to fight corruption. The World Bank supports these efforts and has identified five areas to reduce corruption.

First, corruption must be addressed at the highest levels by making leaders responsible for their actions. This can include placing sanctions, having more candidates for public positions, and making both donations and government meetings open to the public. Second, more involvement by "civil society" participants, like citizen groups and the media, can expose corruption and suggest ways to deal with it. Third, support for more competition and transparency among private businesses can reduce corruption. Fourth, countries should have clear boundaries and restraints within government institutions, especially within the legal system. Last, countries should put in place measures that decrease the possibility of corruption, like independent budget auditing and merit-based systems when promoting employees.

from this project included having 11 million more textbooks, 151 new schools, 2,300 fixed classrooms, more teacher training, and a new Education Management Information System.

As mentioned, the IMF gives loans to countries with balance of payments problems. These countries are unable to pay their bills. Often, they do not have enough funding to raise their standards of living or reduce poverty. Sometimes, countries receiving loans are in need of emergency aid. The IMF offers different financial assistance to member countries:

Loan Name	Purpose	Interest (Cost of Borrowing)	Eligible Countries	Repayment Terms
Extended Credit Facility (ECF)	To help with long-term balance of payments problems	Zero (no extra cost of borrowing money)	Low-income countries	Grace period of 5 ½ years, must be repaid in 10 years
Standby Credit Facility (SCF)	To help with short-term problems, including lending on a precautionary basis (where money is available, but used only if needed)	Zero (no extra cost of borrowing money)	Low-income countries	Grace period of 4 years, must be repaid in 8 years
Rapid Credit Facility (RCF)	To help with immediate balance of payment problems, like to provide emergency funds	Zero (no extra cost of borrowing money)	Low-income countries	Grace period of 5 ½ years, must be repaid in 10 years

Loan Name	Purpose	Interest (Cost of Borrowing)	Eligible Countries	Repayment Terms
Stand-By Arrangements (SBA)	To help with short-term balance of payments problems	Rate of Charge (determined by SDR interest rate)	Middle-income countries (most common way for IMF to help these countries)	Usually repaid in 12–24 months, but must be repaid between 3 ¼ and 5 years
Flexible Credit Line (FCL)	To prevent crises or to respond to a crisis	Rate of Charge (determined by SDR interest rate)	Countries with solid policies that have been carried out	Usually repaid in 12–24 months, but must be repaid between 3 ¼ and 5 years
Precautionary Credit Line (PCL)	Only to prevent a crisis (even without a current balance of payments problem)	Rate of Charge (determined by SDR interest rate)	Open to countries that meet requirements	Line of credit can be renewed in 1–2 years
Extended Fund Facility (EFF)	To help with long-term balance of payments problems that require major policy changes	Rate of Charge (determined by SDR interest rate)	Open to countries that meet requirements	Must be repaid in 4 ½ to 10 years

Both the World Bank and IMF's lending through loans, grants, and credits allows countries to acquire money needed to develop their economies. This development helps improve the quality of life for the people living in these countries. Aid

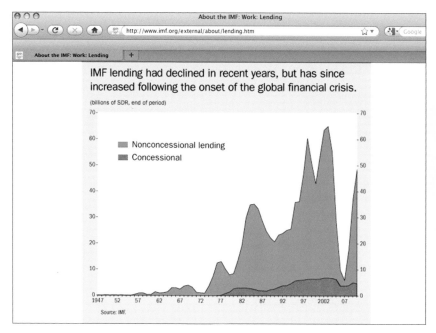

This chart (from www.imf.org) shows the amount of money the IMF has lent to nations around the globe. As one can see, the number fluctuates depending on the health of the world economy.

focuses on both economic and social development. It invests in the people and resources of the country, which lays a foundation for sustainable development. This development generates economic growth because investments put more money into the economy. This growth also reduces poverty, as more people are able to work and afford basic needs. By creating a framework of sustainable economic and social development, both the World Bank and IMF hope to achieve higher standards of living for low- and middle-income countries.

CHAPTER FOUR

IMPACTING GLOBAL ECONOMIES

The World Bank and International Monetary Fund engage in many strategies that affect both national and global economies. An individual country works together with these organizations to encourage economic and social developments. Their combined efforts focus on the needs of a country and its specific goals. Their results, presented in strategy papers, are long-term. For example, goals include investing in the education of young children who will one day contribute to the workforce and investing in more medical treatments that will increase life expectancy in the future. Given the interdependence of the world today, helping one country can greatly impact other economies in the world.

STRATEGIES TO HELP DEVELOPING COUNTRIES

A Poverty Reduction Strategy (PRS) is a report that describes the economic and social development goals for a low-income country. It identifies issues and strategies for poverty reduction,

Ensuring that governments use World Bank and IMF funds for humanitarian aid, like food, clothes, and education, remains a challenge.

as well as the lending required to carry out these strategies. A PRS also states specific targets that track the strategies' effectiveness and encourages integration of the PRS and budget goals. PRSs focus on domestic accountability, including regular government reports, increased monitoring of sectors like health and education, and data on results from poverty reduction programs. Countries are required to prepare PRSs to receive funding at reduced rates (like zero interest) from the IMF and the World Bank.

As of March 2011, the IMF's Executive Fund has received one hundred full Poverty Reduction Strategy Papers (PRSP). The IMF's March 31, 2011, Poverty Reduction Strategy Papers (PRSP) Factsheet notes five PRSP principles. These

Before the 2008 food crisis, 923 million people were undernourished. By 2011, the World Bank was still providing aid for countries most affected by rising food prices.

are (1) countries initiate their own strategies, (2) outcomes focus on poverty reduction, (3) poverty is confronted on many levels, (4) countries work with other governments and organizations (like the World Bank and IMF) to achieve their goals, and (5) poverty reduction is viewed as a long-term goal. Within the PRSP, countries state their goals. As strategies are pursued, progress is tracked.

How the IMF and the World Bank Monitor Countries

Both international organizations monitor the progress of countries that receive their financial assistance. They want to ensure that governments are using the funds for the intended goals and agreed-upon strategies. The World Bank and IMF also want to know if their loans, grants, and credits are resulting in poverty reduction and other beneficial economic and social goals.

Founded in 1973, the Independent Evaluation Group (IEG) assesses the projects funded by the World Bank, the International Finance Corporation, and the Multilateral Investment Guarantee Agency. Then, the IEG's Director-General reports its findings to the board of directors at the World Bank Group. By comparing the original goals and benchmarks to the actual results, the IEG can assess the effectiveness of projects, policies, and procedures. It might even speculate on what would have happened had the funding not occurred. This analysis also provides country and sector comparisons and recommendations for future financial assistance.

Likewise, the IMF monitors the progress of its borrowers through program reviews. It examines the changes in macroeconomic and structural policies of countries receiving financial aid. Countries that receive loans from the IMF must meet certain conditions that allow them to repay the loans so that these funds are available to other countries in the future. Loans are given out in installments, which provide the IMF with leverage. For example, if a country defaults (doesn't repay) its loan, the IMF can withhold any further financial assistance.

For example, the Madagascar Action Plan (the country's PRS) contains eight goals, including an improved infrastructure, more government accountability, increased support for education and health measures (like family planning), and environmentally friendly reforms. Changes that encourage economic growth, higher standards of living, and poverty reduction have been slow to happen. Almost 75 percent of people in this African country still cannot afford basic needs (like food, shelter, and clothing). Improvements in its monitoring process and better integration of the PRS with the budget are needed. Madagascar received most of its investment money from outside sources, such as the World Bank.

Like the PRS, the Country Assistance Strategy (CAS) focuses on what is needed for economic and social development. The World Bank Group develops a CAS by working with political leaders of developing countries and representatives from other sectors, like civil society organizations. The CAS focuses on how the World Bank can help a country reduce poverty. It is the first step in the project cycle.

As discussed, the World Bank provides funding for specific projects in developing countries. After the CAS is prepared, a country and the World Bank figure out goals, risks, and a possible timeframe for the project. Next, the World Bank assesses the country's tools for carrying out the project (like macroeconomic policies), determines the conditions of financial assistance, and monitors the funds. After the money is given out in phases, reports on progress and challenges are given. The final step in this project cycle is a World Bank assessment conducted by the World Bank's Independent Evaluation Group.

Staying Connected

In his book *1493: Uncovering the New World Columbus Created*, Charles C. Mann shows that international transactions can have far-reaching effects. Sometimes, the effects are positive. For example, he cites the tomato plant that was brought from South

Wheat is imported through this Kenyan port in Mombasa. Kenyans depend on this wheat to meet about 65 percent of their domestic consumption.

America to Italy through trade and exploration. In 2008, Italy's tomato crop was $1.4 billion, providing jobs and contributing to economic growth.

By encouraging increased trade, monetary cooperation, and both exchange rate and financial stabilities, the IMF and the World Bank increase the opportunities for different countries to interact with each other. Sometimes, their actions promote the interdependence of countries. Businesses contribute to a growing economy, and many of them rely on foreign markets for consumers, capital, and resources (like labor). They may even rely on foreign countries for trade access.

As mentioned earlier, the World Bank's East Africa Trade and Transport Facilitation Project linked a port in Mombasa, Kenya, with countries located in the interior of Africa (like Uganda). This project did encourage countries, like Uganda, to be dependent on bringing their goods through a Kenyan port. But this access also provided Uganda with an opportunity for economic growth spurred by increased trade.

HELPING DIFFERENT PARTS OF THE ECONOMY: THE WORLD BANK

The project cycle describes the process that countries go through to receive funding for specific World Bank projects. Each project has an effect on national and global economies. Some 2011 projects by the World Bank include:

Project Topic:	Project Goals May Include:	Social and Economic Benefits:	Some Countries with These Project Topics:
Education (Primary, Higher, and Skills Development)	Raising the number of children (especially girls) attending and completing school and providing learning materials	Education allows people to perform higher-skilled jobs. This means they earn more money for consumption of basic goods. This new labor force also contributes to the national economy by producing more goods and services for sale.	**Africa**: Mali, Senegal, and Mozambique **Asia/Pacific**: Pakistan, Vietnam
Health	Proper nutrition, preventing and treating HIV/AIDS and malaria, care for pregnant women and children	Health projects increase life expectancy and improve the quality of life. They also help to create a potential workforce and consumers who can contribute to the economy.	**Africa**: Mali, Nigeria, Kenya, Democratic Republic of Congo **Middle East/North Africa**: Iraq **Latin America/Caribbean**: Argentina, Haiti
Infrastructure	Building up certain sectors, such as energy, mineral, communications, and transportation	Investing in these areas lays the foundation for economic growth, increased employment, and poverty reduction.	**Africa**: Uganda, Malawi, Senegal **Asia**: India, China, and Mongolia
Environment	Investing in areas, including biodiversity, climate change, forest development, air quality management, and water resource management	Preserving natural resources and creating cleaner environments result in both social and economic developments. For example, investments in air quality and water resource management create healthier environments and reduce cleanup costs.	**Africa**: Russia, Indonesia, Mongolia **Latin America/Caribbean**: Argentina, Uruguay, Brazil

Project Topic:	Project Goals May Include:	Social and Economic Benefits:	Some Countries with These Project Topics:
Investment Climate	Creating an investment-friendly environment by providing access to law, reforming the legal system, addressing youth violence, enforcing anti-corruption measures, providing financial management, and encouraging personal and property rights	Encouraging investment boosts economic growth by increasing domestic and foreign investments (access to credit). Investments create jobs, goods, and services, which result in higher standards of living and reductions in poverty.	**Africa:** Kenya, Senegal, Ghana, Mongolia **Middle East/Northern Africa:** Egypt **Latin America/ Caribbean:** Brazil, Peru, Honduras **Asia:** India, Mongolia, Afghanistan
Trade and Integration	Improving efficiency and quality of trade, reducing transport costs, integrating trade regions, improving market access (like roads), and providing financial services (like insurance)	Encouraging trade can stimulate economic growth by increasing exports. It also increases competition because foreign businesses add more goods and services to the markets.	**Africa:** Tanzania, Rwanda, Congo, Kenya **Africa Regions:** African Member States

MYTHS and FACTS

MYTH   Most people in developing countries have enough money to buy basic needs, like food, clothing, and shelter.

FACT   According to the World Bank, "More than half the people in developing countries live on less than $700 a year. Of these, 1.2 billion earn less than $1 a day. As a result, 33,000 children die every day in developing countries."

MYTH   Since there are still poor people in the world, the World Bank and IMF have not made a difference.

FACT   The World Bank and IMF have helped many people in developing countries. For example, the number of people living below the poverty line has decreased, and people are living twenty years longer in the past forty years.

MYTH   The World Bank provides little financial assistance to low-income countries.

FACT   The World Bank (through the IDA) is the largest provider of interest-free loans to low-income countries in the world.

CHAPTER FIVE

PROVIDING EMERGENCY ASSISTANCE

The World Bank and International Monetary Fund work together to help countries face economic challenges, such as persistent poverty and balance of payments problems. These organizations also aid countries in creating an infrastructure that can sustain economic growth and social development. The World Bank provides financial assistance to developing countries, with the poorest countries receiving the most favorable lending conditions.

The IMF offers financial assistance to all members. Sometimes, crises happen, such as natural disasters and severe economic downturns, that result in increased aid to affected areas. At these times, the World Bank and IMF may provide assistance.

RESPONSES TO NATURAL DISASTERS

Both the IMF and the World Bank provide emergency aid to countries affected by natural disasters, such as floods, earthquakes, hurricanes, tsunamis, and droughts. According to the World Bank Group, "3,852 disasters killed more than 780,000 people over the past 10 years, and affected more than 2 billion others and cost a minimum of $960 billion." The World Bank aids countries affected by disasters in several ways, including providing financial assistance, coordinating relief efforts (like when helping those affected by famine in Sudan), and offering strategies for government reforms and rebuilding infrastructures.

The World Bank also analyzes relief efforts to assess the most effective way to help countries rebuild. For example, an Independent Evaluation Group (IEG) report, "WBG Response

Following the 2010 floods in Pakistan, $1 billion by the World Bank and $450 million by the IMF were approved for emergency financing.

to Haiti Earthquake: Evaluative Lessons," found that importing food after a cyclone hit Bangladesh actually hurt domestic rice producers. The IEG suggested that cash assistance for people to buy their own food and coordinating emergency food aid with local food suppliers might have been more effective.

The IMF makes funds available to survivors through the Emergency Natural Disaster Assistance, the Emergency Post-Conflict Assistance, and the Rapid Credit Facility. For example, the IMF has provided emergency aid to Bangladesh and Pakistan after massive floods and to Turkey for earthquake damages. The Dominican Republic, Haiti, Grenada, Dominica, and St. Kitts have received IMF assistance for hurricane damages. Following the earthquake in Haiti in January 2010, the IMF also established the Post-Catastrophe Debt Relief Trust to contribute to international debt relief efforts that help low-income countries suffering from natural disasters.

ASIAN CRISES

In the 1990s, several Asian countries were faced with currency problems. Countries such as South Korea, Malaysia, the Philippines, Singapore, Indonesia, and Taiwan had pegged their currencies to the U.S. dollar, and their economies suffered when the value of the dollar rose. Other factors, including low foreign exchange reserves and speculation, led to massive decreases in the values of these countries' currencies. When their economies fell apart, the IMF provided billions of dollars in loans and coordinated financial assistance with other organizations, including the World Bank and the Asian Development Bank.

In addition, the IMF focused on economic reforms, such as changes in monetary policy aimed at defending the Asian

South Korean employees of Seoulbank, one of the country's most burdened, questioned whether the IMF's plan to increase imports would be beneficial to their business and country.

currencies. As discussed, monetary policy involves using the growth of the money supply (and interest rates) to influence economic performance. Slowing the growth of the money supply and raising interest rates can strengthen a country's currency. Interest is the cost of borrowing money. But, on the flip side, it is also the money earned on investments (like making loans).

Suppose that Malaysia's interest rates rise, which means that foreign investors will earn more money on their investments in Malaysia. This causes more foreign investors to place their money in Malaysia, which also increases the demand (and value) for Malaysian currency. The IMF also advised the Asian countries to adopt banking system reforms and strategies to increase both competition in the marketplace and trade (such as removing barriers). By 2007, many of these Asian countries were running trade surpluses, had built up foreign exchange reserves, and were experiencing economic growth (although not as high as pre-1990 levels).

Global Crisis

At the end of 2007, the world began to feel the effects of the upcoming global crisis. Before long, the world would fall into a recession, with stock markets plummeting, major corporations and banks failing, the housing market collapsing, and lenders reluctant to make loans. In 2009, the IMF predicted that trade would decline by as much as 12 percent. Developing countries dependent on exports suffered, and so did the people who lost their jobs because company sales fell.

In industrialized nations, such as the United States and the United Kingdom, housing prices fell and foreclosures rose during the global financial crisis.

Migrant workers, those working in other countries and sending their earnings back home, were among the millions who lost their jobs. The World Bank predicted a 7 to 10 percent decrease in world remittance flows for 2009. Food and fuel prices also rose, making basic needs more expensive. These price increases had significant effects on those living in poverty.

During the recent global recession, both the IMF and the World Bank provided assistance. The IMF helped countries with financial assistance, raising their monetary resources available for emergency and preventive aid from $250 billion to $750 billion in 2009. Other member countries helped the IMF's efforts. For example, China bought $50 billion in IMF notes (SDRs) to increase the fund's resources. In 2009, the European Union pledged to loan the IMF $100 billion. The IMF provided policy assistance (like recommendations for changes in fiscal and monetary policies) and monitoring and surveillance, and kept track of potential economic challenges.

The World Bank also helped countries weather the recent financial crisis. By 2011, it had given out $81 billion from the agreed-upon $138 billion to member countries in need. According to its site, the seventy-nine poorest countries in the world received $21 billion of this aid. Disbursed money was used for financial and technical assistance, safety net programs (like school lunches), and food. The World Bank set up programs, like the Global Food Crisis Response Program (GFRP), to help people afford basic needs. Established in 2008, the GFRP helps countries affected by rising food prices. By 2011, this program fed almost forty million people in forty-four countries.

In 2010, Greek demonstrators protested government measures intended to reduce spending, such as through public sector wage cuts and job layoffs.

BANKRUPT COUNTRIES

During the recent global recession, Iceland's economy suffered. Three major banks closed, its stock market plummeted (losing more than 80 percent of its value), and the value of its currency (called the krona) fell by over 70 percent. In 2008, Iceland declared bankruptcy. The IMF offered to lend $2.1 billion to Iceland through its Stand-By Arrangement loan program. It disbursed $827 million immediately and agreed to release the rest of the loan in eight installments, subject to IMF review. The IMF also advised on monetary and exchange rate reforms, aimed at stabilizing the krona.

In 2011, Greece also announced that it was bankrupt. The government had borrowed too much money to finance its spending. It owed more money than the whole country produced in goods and services. Its credit rating (trustworthiness in repaying a debt) was also the lowest in the European Union (EU). To help Greece, both the EU and the IMF offered a financial assistance plan. They agreed to provide almost $145 billion, with the IMF offering one-third of this amount through its Stand-By Arrangement loan program. This financial assistance is conditional on both fiscal and monetary reforms. These reforms include reduced government spending, tax increases, less corruption, and increased competition in the marketplace.

CHAPTER SIX

ASSISTANCE IN THE TWENTY-FIRST CENTURY

In the aftermath of the recent global recession, both the IMF and the World Bank have instituted reforms to position themselves more effectively in the twenty-first century. Social developments, new banking practices, and more information have also evolved the goals and direction of these international organizations. From loan packages to anticorruption measures, the World Bank and IMF are implementing new strategies aimed at reducing poverty and creating sustainable economic growth. In 2000, representatives of the World Bank and IMF joined world leaders at the United Nations Millennium Summit to develop the Millennium Development Goals to help the world's poor.

WORLD BANK REFORMS

According to the World Bank's Web site, its reforms focus on "promoting inclusiveness, innovations, efficiency, effectiveness,

The World Bank's "Let's Talk Development" blog (http://blogs.worldbank.org) provides a forum to discuss and debate economic development and poverty reduction. Topics include the role of government in developing economies and field reports.

and accountability." Inclusiveness applies to both the World Bank structure and its project goals. For example, the World Bank increased the representation and voting power of developing countries, like adding a seat for a sub-Saharan representative. The "WDR 2012: Gender Equality and Development" tracks gender equality in development projects, such as the number of women who own land, go to school, and receive medical treatment.

Together, the World Bank and Science, Technology and Innovation (STI) identify, develop, and carry out innovative strategies to promote economic and social development. They encourage the use of technology to create local business opportunities and train workers for the twenty-first century. To address efficiency, the World Bank continues to fund projects that promote transparency. Full disclosure of information can lead to a more efficient use of resources.

The Independent Evaluation Group (IEG) continues to assess the effectiveness of the World Bank's performance. In its 2010 report, "Results and Performance of the World Bank Group," the IEG found some areas of concern, including declines in health, population, and transportation compared to long-term trends. The Communication for Governance and

Accountability Program at the World Bank also promotes better accountability by encouraging the use of communication to bring together individuals, civic society, the government, and media.

Finally, the World Bank continues to stress the connection between corruption and poverty. In its 2011 report, entitled "Curbing Fraud, Corruption, and Collusion in the Roads Sector," the World Bank found that the poor suffer the most from corrupt behaviors in the transportation sector. This occurs because they lose the most from missed economic and social opportunities. The World Bank researches the effects of corruption on its project topics (like transportation) and focuses on decreasing corruption in areas directly related to its project goals.

IMF REFORMS

In a 2009 CRS report for Congress entitled "The Global Financial Crisis: Increasing IMF Resources and the Role of Congress," Jonathan E. Sanford and Martin A. Weiss wrote, "The recent financial crisis has also enhanced the IMF's role in crisis management and given it a key place in current efforts to reform the world financial system." The recent economic challenges have strengthened and redefined the IMF's goals in several ways.

First, the IMF reformed its loan process, including offering individualized loan terms. By March 2011, the IMF increased crisis lending to $250 billion, which is the highest level in IMF history. Most loans that deal with the effects of crises are Stand-By Arrangements. The IMF also added two new lines of

The First Woman in Charge of the IMF

In 2011, Christine Lagarde became the first woman to head the International Monetary Fund. As France's former finance minister, she is the eleventh European to be in charge of the IMF. After becoming the managing director, Lagarde stated her intent to bring diversity to the IMF in terms of race, gender, culture, and academic background. She also wants more inclusion of emerging markets.

One of Lagarde's main focuses for the IMF is economic recovery from the recent financial crisis, including job creation and increased consumer demand. In an August 2011 conference of central bankers in Jackson Hole, Wyoming, Lagarde mentioned her support for more financial assistance for American homeowners and more capital for European banks. The IMF managing director serves a five-year term.

credit (ways to receive loans): the Flexible Credit Line (FCL) and the Precautionary Credit Line. As of March 2011, only Poland, Mexico, and Colombia had access to FLC funds but had not used them.

Second, the IMF has become even more instrumental in providing policy suggestions and forecasts. It collects information on potential risks to the financial system and how policies in one country can affect economic performances in others. The IMF has also made suggestions to address global regulations.

Many member countries, especially industrialized nations, have used this information.

MILLENNIUM DEVELOPMENT GOALS

In 2000, 189 countries came together to develop the Millennium Development Goals (MDGs). Within the framework of the United Nations, the international community is working together to promote human development by pursuing eight goals: (1) reducing poverty and hunger, (2) promoting education, (3) encouraging gender equality and empowerment of women, (4) fighting diseases (like HIV/AIDS and malaria), (5) decreasing child deaths, (6) allowing women to give birth with fewer life-threatening risks, (7) promoting environmental sustainability (like having enough drinkable water), and (8) creating a global community that works together to achieve social and economic development (including job creation).

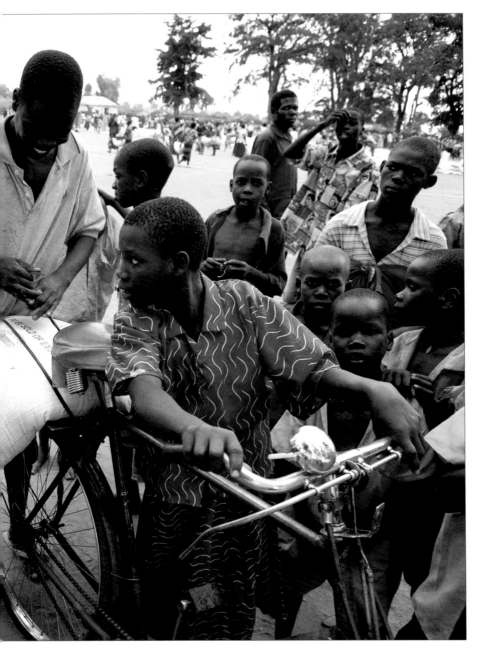

Thousands of Africans who live with HIV/AIDS depend on food programs supported by international organizations, such as the World Bank.

Both the World Bank and the IMF are part of these efforts. Through its work, the World Bank advances these goals for development, particularly in middle- to low-income countries. Through financial and technical assistance, the IMF also supports the Millennium Development Goals. The process for social and economic development in poor countries has been a slow one. It has also been made worse by recent climate, food, and economic crises. But international organizations, such as the World Bank and the IMF, continue their efforts toward poverty reduction and social and economic development.

GLOSSARY

accountability Being held responsible for something.

balance of payments A record of international transactions, which includes the current account, capital account, and financial account.

corruption Dishonest behavior by people in power, usually for gain.

developing countries Nations with low-to-middle standards of living.

economic growth Increase in the amount of goods and services that can be produced over consecutive time periods.

exchange rate policy A country's management of the value of its currency compared to other currencies in the world.

financial assistance Money-related aid (like a loan).

financial stability Managing money-related risks without significantly impacting economic performance.

fiscal policy Government use of spending or tax policies to affect economic performance.

infrastructure Basic framework needed for a community to function (like roads and water lines).

interest rate The cost of borrowing money or return on investment.

international monetary cooperation Countries working together in matters that involve money.

international trade Exchange of goods, services, and capital between countries.

investment Something that people put their money into (like stocks, bonds, real estate) in hopes of earning more money in the future.

loan Borrowed money to be repaid under certain conditions.

market economy Supply and demand for goods and services that drive the economy.

monetary policy The central bank's use of the money supply and interest rates to influence economic performance.

poverty line A classification that involves minimum income required to afford basic needs, like food and shelter.

standard of living The comfort level that people experience from having goods and services available to them.

sustainable development Able to meet the needs in the present and the future.

FOR MORE INFORMATION

CARE USA
151 Ellis Street NE
Atlanta, GA 30303
(404) 681-2552
Web site: http://www.care.org
One of the largest relief organizations, CARE began by
    helping World War II refugees. Later, it shifted its focus
    to helping the world's poor.

International Finance Corporation
2121 Pennsylvania Avenue NW
Washington, DC 20433
(202) 473-3800
Web site: http://www.ifc.org
As a member of the World Bank Group, the International
    Finance Corporation reduces poverty by promoting
    competitive markets in developing countries,
    encouraging cooperation between companies and private
    sector partners, promoting employment opportunities,
    and facilitating financial assistance.

International Institute for Sustainable Development
161 Portage Avenue East, 6th Floor

Winnipeg, MB R3B 0Y4
Canada
(204) 958-7700
Web site: http://www.iisd.org
The International Institute for Sustainable Development
encourages sustainable development through innovation,
partnerships, research, and communications. It works
with business leaders, governments, and nongovernment
organizations around the world.

International Monetary Fund (IMF)
700 19th Street NW
Washington, DC 20431
(202) 623-7000
Web site: http://www.imf.org
The International Monetary Fund encourages monetary
cooperation, international trade, financial and exchange
rate stability, and economic growth with poverty
reduction. It uses surveillance, financial assistance, and
technical assistance to achieve its goals.

Multilateral Investment Guarantee Agency
World Bank Group
1818 H Street NW
Washington, DC 20433
(202) 458-2538
Web site: http://www.miga.org
As a member of the World Bank Group, the Multilateral
Investment Guarantee Agency promotes foreign direct
investment in developing countries by protecting against
noncommercial risks.

United Nations
402 East 42nd Street
New York, NY 10017
(212) 355-4165
Web site: http://www.un.org
The United Nations officially works to maintain peace,
promote international cooperation, and promote
economic and social development.

World Bank
1818 H Street NW
Washington, DC 20433
(202) 473-1000
Web site: http://www.worldbank.org
The World Bank is made up of the International Bank of
Reconstruction and Development (IBRD) and the
International Development Association (IDA). Through
its development policy and investment funding, the
World Bank encourages economic and social
development and poverty reduction.

WEB SITES

Due to the changing nature of Internet links, Rosen Publishing
has developed an online list of Web sites related to the subject
of this book. This site is updated regularly. Please use this link
to access the list:

http://www.rosenlinks.com/rwe/wrld

FOR FURTHER READING

Battaile Jr., William G. *The Poverty Reduction Strategy Initiative: Findings from Ten Country Case Studies of World Bank and IMF Support.* Washington, DC: World Bank Publications, 2005.

Boughton, James. M., and Domenico Lombardi. *Finance, Development, and the IMF.* Oxford, UK: Oxford University Press, 2009.

Brau, Eduard, and Ian McDonald. *Successes of the International Monetary Fund: Untold Stories of Cooperation at Work.* Basingstoke, UK: Palgrave Macmillan, 2009.

Buira, Ariel. *Reforming the Governance of the IMF and the World Bank.* New York, NY: Anthem Press, 2006.

Caprio, Gerard, Jonathan L. Fiechter, Robert E. Litan, and Michael Pomerleano. *The Future of State-owned and Financial Institutions* (World Bank/IMF/Brookings Emerging Market). Washington, DC: The Brookings Institution, 2004.

Copelovitch, Mark S. *The International Monetary Fund in the Global Economy.* Cambridge, UK: Cambridge University Press, 2010.

Dener, Cem, William Leslie Dorotinsky, and Joanne Watkins. *Financial Management Informational Systems: 25 Years of World Bank Experience on What Works and What Doesn't*

(World Bank Studies). Washington, DC: World Bank Publications, 2011.

Gould, Erica. *Money Talks: The International Monetary Fund, Conditionality and Supplementary Financiers.* Palo Alto, CA: Stanford University Press, 2006.

Harris, Clive. *Private Participation in Infrastructure in Developing Countries: Trends, Impacts, and Policy Lessons* (World Bank Working Papers). Washington, DC: World Bank Publications, 2003.

Humphreys, Norman K., and Sarah Tenney. *Historical Dictionary of the International Monetary Fund.* Lanham, MD: Scarecrow Press, 2011.

Kenen, Peter B. *Reform of the International Monetary Fund.* Washington, DC: Council on Foreign Relations Press, 2007.

Kosack, Stephen, Gustav Ranis, and James Raymond Vreeland. *Globalization and the Nation State: The Impact of the IMF and the World Bank.* Abingdon, UK: Routledge, 2006.

Marshall, Katherine. *The World Bank: From Reconstruction to Development to Equity.* Abingdon, UK: Routledge, 2008.

Paloni, Alberto, and Maurizio Zanardi. *The IMF, World Bank and Policy Reform.* Abingdon, UK: Routledge, 2006.

Panickaveetil, Stanley Cleetus. *World Bank and Beyond: Memoir and a Proposal.* Kensington, MD: Programming and Budgeting Corporation, 2007.

Park, Susan, and Antje Vetterlein. *Owning Development: Creating Policy Norms in the IMF and the World Bank.* Cambridge, UK: Cambridge University Press, 2010.

Vreeland, James Raymond. *The International Monetary Fund (IMF): Politics of Conditional Lending* (Global Institutions). Abingdon, UK: Routledge, 2012.

Woods, Ngaire. *The Globalizers: The IMF, the World Bank, and Their Borrowers*. Ithaca, NY: Cornell University Press, 2007.

World Bank. *World Bank*. Washington, DC: World Bank Publications, 2007.

World Bank. *World Development Report 2011: Conflict, Security, and Development*. Washington, DC: World Bank Publications, 2011.

World Bank. *World Development Report 2012: Gender Equality and Development*. Washington, DC: World Bank Publications, 2011.

BIBLIOGRAPHY

Anderson, Camilla. "Iceland Gets Help to Recover from Historic Crisis." International Monetary Fund, December 2, 2008. Retrieved June 2011 (http://www.imf.org/external/pubs/ft/survey/so/2008/INT111908A.htm).

Driscoll, David. "The IMF and the World Bank: How Do They Differ?" International Monetary Fund. Retrieved June 2011 (http://www.imf.org/external/pubs/ft/exrp/differ/differ.htm).

Hollander, Barbara. *How Credit Crises Happen*. New York, NY: Rosen Publishing, 2011.

Hollander, Barbara. *How Currency Devaluation Works*. New York, NY: Rosen Publishing, 2011.

International Monetary Fund. "A Changing IMF: Responses to the Crisis." March 16, 2011. Retrieved June 2011 (http://www.imf.org/external/np/exr/facts/changing.htm).

International Monetary Fund. "How the IMF Promotes Global Economic Stability." August 29, 2011. Retrieved September 2011 (http://www.imf.org/external/np/exr/facts/globstab.htm).

International Monetary Fund. "IMF Emergency Assistance: Supporting Recovery from Natural Disasters and Armed Conflicts." September 15, 2011. Retrieved September 2011 (http://www.imf.org/external/np/exr/facts/conflict.htm).

International Monetary Fund. "Poverty Reduction Strategy Papers (PRSP)." September 14, 2011. Retrieved June 2011 (http://www.imf.org/external/np/exr/facts/prsp.htm).

Karmin, Craig. *Biography of the Dollar.* New York, NY: Three Rivers Press, 2009.

New York Times. "Christine Lagarde's Tough Message." August 30, 2011. Retrieved September 2011 (http://www.nytimes.com/2011/08/31/opinion/christine-lagardes-tough-message.html).

RTE News/Business. "French MPs Agree to Greece Rescue Plan." September 7, 2011. Retrieved September 2011 (http://www.rte.ie/news/2011/0907/greece-business.html).

United Nations Development Programme. "Millennium Development Goals." Retrieved July 2011 (http://www.beta.undp.org/undp/en/home/mdgoverview.html).

Vision 2020: Equality in Sight. "Conducting the IMF." July 11, 2011. Retrieved August 2011 (http://equalityinsight.wordpress.com/2011/07/11/conducting-the-imf).

Vreeland, James Raymond. *The IMF and Economic Development.* Cambridge, UK: Cambridge University Press, 2003.

World Bank Group. "About Anti-Corruption." Retrieved July 2011 (http://web.worldbank.org/WBSITE/EXTERNAL/TOPICS/EXTPUBLICSECTORANDGOVERNANCE/EXTANTICORRUPTION/0,,contentMDK:21540659~menuPK:384461~pagePK:148956~piPK:216618~theSitePK:384455,00.html).

World Bank Group. "About IEG." Independent Evaluation Group. Retrieved July 2011 (http://ieg.worldbankgroup.org/content/ieg/en/home/about.html).

World Bank Group. "Africa." Retrieved June 2011 (http://web.worldbank.org/WBSITE/EXTERNAL/COUNTRIES/

AFRICAEXT/0,,menuPK:258649~pagePK:158889~pi
PK:146815~theSitePK:258644,00.html).

World Bank Group. "Aid for Trade: World Bank Transport
Facilitation Project Boosts Trade in East Africa."
Retrieved July 2011 (http://web.worldbank.org/
WBSITE/EXTERNAL/TOPICS/TRADE/0,,content
MDK:22960919~pagePK:210058~piPK:210062~theSite
PK:239071,00.html).

World Bank Group. "Country and Lending Groups."
Retrieved June 2011 (http://data.worldbank.org/about/
country-classifications/country-and-lending-groups#
East_Asia_and_Pacific).

World Bank Group. "Financial Crisis." Retrieved June
2011 (http://www.worldbank.org/financialcrisis/
bankinitiatives.htm).

World Bank Group. "Food Crisis." Retrieved June 2011 (http://
www.worldbank.org/foodcrisis/bankinitiatives.htm).

World Bank Group. "Glossary." Retrieved July 2011 (http://
www.worldbank.org/depweb/english/beyond/global/
glossary.html).

World Bank Group. "GNI per capita 2010, Atlas Method and
PPP." Retrieved June 2011 (http://siteresources.worldbank.
org/DATASTATISTICS/Resources/GNIPC.pdf).

World Bank Group. "How We Classify Countries." Retrieved
June 2011 (http://data.worldbank.org/about/country-
classifications).

World Bank Group. "An Introduction to IEG for First Time
Visitors." Retrieved July 2011 (http://www.worldbank.
org/ieg/intro).

World Bank Group. "Leveraging Trade for Development and
Inclusive Growth: The World Bank Group Trade

Strategy for 2011–2021." June 10, 2011. Retrieved July 2011 (http://siteresources.worldbank.org/TRADE/Resources/WBGTradeStrategyJune10.pdf).

World Bank Group. "Natural Disasters." Retrieved July 2011 (http://www.worldbank.org/ieg/naturaldisasters).

World Bank Group. "Road Sector Looks to Curb Fraud, Corruption, and Collusion." Retrieved July 2011 (http://web.worldbank.org/WBSITE/EXTERNAL/NEWS/0,,contentMDK:22928222~menuPK:34457~pagePK:34370~piPK:34424~theSitePK:4607,00.html).

World Bank Group. "World Bank Reform." Retrieved July 2011 (http://www.worldbank.org/html/extdr/worldbankreform).

INDEX

About the Author

Barbara Gottfried Hollander has authored several economics and business books, including *How Currency Devaluation Works*; *How Credit Crises Happen*; *Money Matters: An Introduction to Economics*; *Booms, Bubbles and Busts: The Economic Cycle*; *Managing Money*; *Raising Money*; and *Paying for College: Practical, Creative Strategies*. She was the economics editor of the *World Almanac and Book of Facts* and is both an economic content developer and specialized project manager for companies that provide online education programs. Hollander received a B.A. in economics from the University of Michigan and an M.A. in economics from New York University, specializing in statistics and econometrics and international economics.

Photo Credits

Cover, p. 18 Shutterstock.com, cover (headline) © www.istockphoto.com/ Lilli Day; p. 5 Tim Sloan/AFP/Getty Images; pp. 7, 15, 28, 38, 48, 57 Mario Tama/Getty Images; p. 8 Alfred Eisenstaedt/Time & Life Pictures/ Getty Images; p. 11 Alex Wong/Getty Images; pp. 13, 58–59 The World Bank; p. 14 Fabrice Coffrini/AFP/Getty Images; p. 16 Justin Sullivan/ Getty Images; p. 22–23 © AP Images; p. 24 Farooq Naeem/AFP/Getty Images; pp. 29, 43, 52–53 Bloomberg/Bloomberg via Getty Images; p. 33 AFP/AFP/Getty Images; p. 37 IMF; p. 39 STR/AFP/Getty Images; p. 40 Alexander Joe/AFP/Getty Images; p. 49 Carl de Souza/AFP/Getty Images; pp. 50–51 Choo Youn-Kong/AFP/Getty Images; p. 55 Aris Messins/AFP/Getty Images; pp. 62–63 Jean-Marc Giboux/Getty Images; cover and interior graphic elements: © www.istockphoto.com/Andrey Prokhorov (front cover), © www.istockphoto.com/Dean Turner (back cover and interior pages) © www.istockphoto.com/Darja Tokranova; www. istockphoto.com/articular (27); © www.istockphoto.com/studiovision (pp. 65, 67, 70, 73, 77); © www.istockphoto.com/Chen Fu Soh (multiple interior pages).

Designer: Nicole Russo; Editor: Nicholas Croce;
Photo Researcher: Marty Levick